Making Sense of Benefits

ACKNOWLEDGEMENTS

We are extremely grateful to Peter Alcock of Sheffield Hallam University for his submission to the Commission which formed the basis of the discussion from which this paper is drawn.

PREFACE

The Commission on Social Justice was established at the instigation of John Smith MP, Leader of the Labour Party, at the end of 1992. Chaired by Sir Gordon Borrie QC, the Commission's goal is to develop a new social and economic vision for the United Kingdom, backed up by practical policies, particularly in the fields of employment, taxation and social welfare.

In July 1993, the Commission published two discussion papers which summed up the first phase of our work. *The Justice Gap* sets out the Commission's working definition of 'social justice' and documents the extent of injustice in the United Kingdom today. *Social Justice in a Changing World* analyses the social, economic and political revolutions which have taken place since William Beveridge devised the social insurance system 50 years ago, and sets out objectives for policy.

For the next phase of our work – identifying and evaluating policy options – the Commission has divided into three Panels dealing with work and wages; money and wealth; and communities and services. Over the next six months, we will publish a series of issues papers explaining some of the tough questions which we believe the country faces; setting out the advantages and disadvantages of different options; and inviting responses.

These issues papers do not represent the Commission's views, for the simple reason that neither the Panels nor the Commission as a whole has yet reached policy conclusions. Nor do they argue one particular case. They are designed instead to promote debate and thereby to assist us in reaching well-informed conclusions later in our work.

Making Sense of Benefits has been prepared by the Commission's staff and is designed to provide a simple guide to an increasingly complicated system of benefits, tax reliefs and private provision. In particular, it aims to cut through the confused – and confusing – debate about 'universal' versus 'targeted' benefits. Because both terms have been so abused, we propose to abandon their use completely and to describe benefits more precisely as 'contributory' (based on National Insurance contributions); 'means tested' (based on a test of income and savings); or 'categorical' (benefits awarded to a particular group of people, without a test of either contributions or means.)

Defining our terms precisely is more than a semantic issue. As the comparisons we make with other countries illustrate, every benefits system in a modern industrialised country is a mixture of categorical, contributory and means-tested benefits. A new report by John Hills, 'The Future of Welfare: a guide to the debate' (1993) from the Joseph Rowntree Foundation, likewise stresses that policy-makers need to choose from a range of possible measures. The question facing the nation (as well as the Commission) is what the fairest and most efficient mix of benefits is: and that question cannot be reduced to a simplistic choice between 'universalism' and 'targeting'.

An earlier paper in this series looked in detail at the strengths and weaknesses of the contributory principle as a basis for benefits. Other papers will consider issues such as full employment and family policy (including the future of child benefit) which are also central to the Commission's work.

November 1993

INTRODUCTION

There is widespread confusion about the different kinds of social security benefits which exist in Britain today. The term 'universal' is now widely used to describe quite different benefits such as **child benefit** (which is neither means-tested nor based on contributions, although it is based on a residence test) and the **retirement pension** (which is based on national insurance contributions, not on a test of means or residence). In order to clarify the debate about the future of benefits, it is essential to have a clear definition of each kind of benefit.

In practice, the welfare state of almost every industrialised country is based on a mix of different kinds of benefit. Benefits can be classified according to their **purpose** or according to the **basis** on which they are awarded. In terms of purpose, some benefits are designed to provide an income during periods of our life when we cannot rely on earnings. Others are designed to help meet additional costs faced by some groups of people at every income level (eg child benefit), while others are designed to relieve poverty (eg income support). In terms of the basis of payment, some benefits are based on national insurance contributions; others are means-tested; a third group are neither means-tested nor contributions-tested.

Benefits are usually thought of as being provided in cash. Tax allowances and reliefs, however, have exactly the same effect on public finance as cash benefits, even though the public accounting system does not acknowledge that at present. In order to get an accurate picture of the state's financial provision for people, benefits and tax allowances must be considered together.

In addition to benefits and tax allowances, various forms of private provision can help to protect people against risks and spread income across their lives. A growing proportion of older people, for instance, have occupational pensions in addition to the national insurance pension. But private provision is not independent of government policy. The extensive tax reliefs available for occupational and private pensions and for pre-1984 life insurance policies means that taxpayers are helping to finance much of the provision which is seen as purely 'private'. Furthermore, government helps to dictate what kinds of private provision are available, directly in its role as regulator, indirectly by determining how adequate or inadequate public provision is.

This paper looks, first, at the objectives which we think any benefits system should serve; and second, at the different kinds of financial provision – both public and private – which exist today in the United Kingdom and some other countries.

OBJECTIVES

A benefits and tax allowance system has to serve many different objectives. The Commission believes that the system of benefits, tax allowances and private provision, taken together, should:

- prevent poverty wherever possible, and alleviate it where necessary;

- protect people against risks, labour market failures and other contingencies (including unpaid caring work);

- redistribute resources over individuals' life-cycle;

- redistribute resources from richer to poorer members of society;

- redistribute resources to those with children;

- promote social cohesion.

There are also a number of criteria by which the operation of these systems should be judged. The systems should:

- create no disincentive to taking paid work;

- be simple and comprehensible;

- enhance women's independence;

- be economically sustainable, with revenue and expenditure balanced;

- be citizen centred, responsive to people's demands and needs;

- be effective and cost-effective;

- be fair, treating equal needs equally, and not discriminating against people on grounds such as race, religion, sex, disability or sexual orientation;

- be flexible, able to adapt to changing individual and social needs.

Inevitably, objectives conflict and a scheme which rates well on some criteria may fail on others. But unless policy-makers are clear about both objectives and criteria, debate about different policy mixes will be inadequate.

The benefits system in the UK is commonly thought of as redistributing resources from rich to poor. But recent research from the London School of Economics has shown that the most important effect of the UK welfare state (including the NHS and other services as well as taxes and benefits) is to redistribute resources across people's own lifecycles (Fallingham *et al*, 1993). About 60 per cent of benefits are paid for by the recipient's own contributions and relevant tax payments; the remainder represent redistribution from richer to poorer and from men to women. Furthermore, the tax reliefs given to occupational pensions, mortgage interest payments and so on involve a redistribution from poorer to richer – although this is not their objective.

CLASSIFYING BENEFITS ACCORDING TO PAYMENT CONDITIONS

The most common way of classifying benefits is to look at the conditions for payments. Politicians and commentators regularly pose a choice between 'universal' and 'targeted' benefits – in other words, non means-tested and means-tested – with those on the right favouring a shift towards targeting and those on the left usually defending universality. But this simple dualism will not do, either to describe the present complex system of benefits or to analyse how we might move forward.

The idea of 'universality' suggests a benefit paid to everyone regardless of need, circumstances, previous contributions or current resources. No such benefit exists in the United Kingdom today. Even child benefit (which, of course, is only paid in respect of children) is not payable for children who have been in local authority care for more than eight weeks, nor for children who are living abroad (other than temporarily) even though the parents are settled here.

A 'basic income' or 'citizen's income' (championed by some as an alternative to the present tax and benefits system) could properly be described as 'universal' – although even a citizen's income would require a definition of who the 'citizens' were who would receive it. Given the state of the UK's citizenship laws, this would not be an easy task, and supporters of citizen's income usually prefer a test of residence (which might itself give rise to difficulties within the European Community). As far as the present benefits system goes, the Commission intends to use precise terms to describe different varieties of non-means-tested benefits and will abandon the use of the term 'universal' completely. We hope that we can encourage others to do the same.

Although 'targeting' has come to mean 'means-testing,' there is no reason why it should be confined in this way. Benefits can clearly be 'targeted' through criteria other than income, age being an obvious alternative. Given the confusion which has arisen with this term, however, we will abandon its use too. This is not simply a matter of terminology: the choice before us is not a crude one between means-tested and non-means-tested benefits, but a complex one between a wide variety of different kinds of provision.

We classify benefits into the following groups:

- **contributory** (based on a test of national insurance contributions paid or credited)

- **means-tested** (based on a test of income and assets)

- **categorical** (neither means-tested nor contributions-tested)

- **occupational** (based on employment)

- **discretionary**

This classification needs to be qualified by noting that all benefits are 'categorical' in the sense that they only go to a defined category of people. The retirement pension, while requiring national insurance contributions, is also based on age (although, despite its name, it is no longer based on a retirement test). And to claim Family Credit you must be in work and have children, as well as demonstrating through a means-test that your income is insufficient. In our classification, categorical benefits are defined as those which only have a categorical test of eligibility (eg. child benefit).

Contributory (national insurance) benefits

The centrepiece of the Beveridge Report was a comprehensive scheme of social insurance designed to rationalise the different insurance systems which had grown up in the first half of the century, and to provide an adequate benefit when the contributor's earning power was interrupted or destroyed. Contributory benefits include national insurance unemployment benefit, sickness benefit, widow's pension and the retirement pension. Eligibility for such benefits depends upon having paid enough national insurance contributions during previous periods of employment.

Contributions conditions have become increasingly onerous in the last decade; as a result of that and other factors, such as the growth in long-term unemployment, fewer than half of the unemployed actually receive unemployment benefit. Because married women were previously allowed to opt for reduced national insurance contributions, and because of the absence until recently of home responsibilities protection, it will not be until 2014 that all women will have some (not necessarily full) entitlement to a national insurance pension in their own right. We discuss the pros and cons of a contributory-based social insurance system in a separate paper (Bennett, 1993).

Means-tested benefits

Means-tested benefits are paid to people in specified circumstances whose family's total income and assets fall below a certain level. In the UK, the most important means-tested benefits are income support and housing benefit; in addition, some means-tested benefits are provided in kind (free school meals, prescriptions and so on) to those receiving income support. These are often known as 'passported' benefits. (Free prescriptions are also, of course, available on a non-means tested basis to children, pensioners and some other groups.) Other means-tested benefits include council tax benefit, family credit and the disability working allowance.

Means-tested benefits are designed to fulfil different functions. For instance, income support is designed to provide a minimum income for people with little or no employment or other income. Family credit, by contrast, is designed to supplement low wages, as is the disability working allowance. Housing benefit helps to meet rental costs both for those not in employment and for those on low wages. Means-tested benefits of various kinds have become increasingly important over the last decade.

Categorical benefits

Categorical benefits are paid to people in certain defined circumstances, without a test of previous contributions or means. The best known such benefit is perhaps child benefit, which is payable in respect of almost all children living in the UK under the age of 16 and unmarried people under the age of 19 who are receiving full-time secondary education. Many disability-related benefits also fall into this category, including industrial injury benefits for people injured in an industrial accident or suffering from a prescribed industrial disease; and the disability living allowance. The invalid care allowance, also paid without test of means or contributions, is available to people who are caring for people receiving certain disability benefits.

Tax allowances and reliefs are the equivalent, within the tax system, of categorical benefits. Personal tax allowances are not means-tested, except in the sense that people with incomes below the level of the tax allowance do not fully benefit from them, and higher-rate taxpayers get a greater benefit from the allowance than standard-rate taxpayers. Child benefit (usually paid to mothers) was designed to replace the child allowance which used to be available (usually to fathers) through the tax system. The tax relief on mortgage interest payments goes to all taxpayers with a mortgage, regardless of their means. Tax allowances to taxpayers who are registered as blind are a recognition of the extra costs which blindness entails, taking the form of tax relief rather than a cash payment. As these examples suggest, tax allowances can – like cash benefits – serve a range of different functions; but – unlike cash benefits – they are available by definition only to those who pay income tax.

Occupational benefits

Most occupational benefits – such as occupational pension schemes – depend upon the discretion of employers and will therefore be discussed later (see page 11 below). But there are also two statutory, occupational benefits, statutory sick pay and statutory maternity pay. Both benefits are only available to employees – people with the appropriate form of employment contract – who meet other qualifying conditions. Neither benefit is means-tested and neither depends directly upon having paid national insurance contributions.

Discretionary benefits

In 1987/8, the government established a Social Fund to replace the previous system of lump sum payments to supplementary benefit (now income support) recipients. Fund payments or loans are means-tested; they are only available to people on low incomes. But, with the exception of grants for maternity expenses, funeral expenses and periods of cold weather, Social Fund payments are also discretionary. Claimants have no legal entitlement to such payments, most of which are made in the form of loans.

PRIVATE PROVISION

The system of benefits and tax allowances is only part of the story. Particularly when it comes to retirement, the UK has a 'mixed economy' of benefit provision. Private provision is, however, more restricted in its nature than the benefits system. It consists of occupational provision, private pensions, insurance policies, private savings and charity.

Occupational welfare

The most important occupational provision comes from occupational pension schemes, which cover about half of all employees (57 per cent of employed men, 37 per cent of employed women). Like the national insurance retirement pension, occupational pensions are based on the contributions record built up while in employment. Unlike national insurance benefits, which are paid for out of current revenue, occupational pensions are paid for out of the investment fund generated by previous contributions. When pension schemes provide a defined benefit (usually related to final salary), they include a substantial hidden element of cross-subsidy, particularly from those who leave the scheme early to those who remain until retirement.

Occupational welfare is, however, wider than pension schemes. Some employers, for instance, provide paid maternity and sick leave well beyond that required by law; a few provide paid paternity leave as well.

Others offer their employees low-interest rate loans or mortgages, free private medical insurance and other benefits.

Private pensions

About five million people are now contributing to personal pensions which have expanded rapidly in the last few years, encouraged by the substantial tax relief and national insurance contribution rebates provided by the present government. Although there are arguments about the level of earnings needed before a personal pension scheme is worthwhile, it is generally accepted that they are unlikely to be suitable for most men and women earning below £8,000 – £9,000 a year.

Private Insurance

The private insurance market enables people to make further provision against contingencies which are also covered by the benefits system – such as sickness or invalidity – as well as to protect themselves against risks which are not covered at all by the state. Obviously, insurance only protects those who can afford to pay the premium: in 1990 over half of the population were unable to save £10 a week and/or to insure the contents of their homes. Furthermore, some risks like unemployment are not suited to the technical conditions of the private insurance market (Barr, 1988).

Charity

The private equivalent to the discretionary Social Fund is charity. The financial help provided to low-income families by charities has become increasingly important in recent years, as public resources have become less adequate. As with the discretionary element of the Social Fund, however, those in need have no entitlement to charitable help.

Diagram 1 (overleaf) provides a 'map' of financial provision in the UK, using the classifications discussed above. It is not designed to be comprehensive, but examples are given in each category to illustrate the benefits available.

DIAGRAM 1
A 'MAP' OF FINANCIAL PROVISION IN THE UK

PUBLIC	PRIVATE

CATEGORICAL
 	
eg Child benefit
    Disbability living allowance
    Personal tax allowance
	—

CONTRIBUTORY/SOCIAL INSURANCE
 	
eg Unemployment benefit
    Widow's pension
    Retirement pension
	CONTRIBUTORY/PRIVATE INSURANCE
	
	eg Mortgage protection
	    Life insurance
	    Personal pension

OCCUPATIONAL
 	
    Statutory sick pay
    Statutory maternity leave
	OCCUPATIONAL
	
	eg Occupation pensions
	    Sick pay

MEANS-TESTED
 	
    Income support
    Housing benefit
    Family credit
	—

DISCRETIONARY
 	
    Social Fund
	DISCRETIONARY
	
	    Charity

CLASSIFYING BENEFITS
ACCORDING TO PURPOSE

So far, we have looked at benefits and tax allowances, and at private provision according to the basis on which they are paid. As we said earlier, this is the focus of most of the present debate. But it is at least as important to classify benefits according to their purpose. There are three main purposes of financial provision:

● earnings replacement

● meeting extra costs

● relief of poverty

State benefits designed to replace earnings include unemployment benefit; sickness benefit and statutory sick pay; maternity allowance and statutory maternity pay; invalidity benefit, severe disablement allowance and invalid care allowance; and retirement pensions. Occupational pensions, together with employers' maternity and sick pay, personal pensions and mortgage protection schemes are similarly designed to replace earnings. Particularly among people who are self-employed, there is a growing interest in private insurance against the risk of sickness or long-term disability.

Some benefits are designed not to replace earnings but to meet the extra costs associated with particular circumstances. Child benefit clearly falls into this category, although it is sometimes discussed as if its sole purpose is (or should be) to relieve poverty. Disability living allowance, attendance allowance and industrial injuries benefits are designed at least in part to meet the additional needs caused by different disabilities. For this reason, they can be paid on top of a benefit designed to replace earnings or to relieve poverty.

Much private insurance is designed to enable individuals to protect themselves against risks such as burglary, fire and accidents. In effect, policies of this kind allow people to meet most or all of the extra costs incurred in such an eventuality through the insurance payment, rather than having to draw on their earnings or savings.

Benefits intended to relieve poverty include all the means-tested benefits – although there is, of course, dispute about how effectively they achieve their purpose. But non-means tested benefits may also have, as one of their objectives, the relief of poverty. When William Beveridge proposed national insurance retirement pensions, he did so in the knowledge that retirement in the 1930s usually meant poverty. Thus, the retirement pension, available to contributors without a test of means, was an effective method of relieving poverty as well as replacing earnings. Today's non-contributory pension for people over the age of 80 with no other retirement pension is also designed to relieve poverty within an age-group where a very high proportion live on low incomes (although at only £33.90 a week, it is still below the income support and housing benefit levels.)

Diagram 2 gives a second 'map' of benefits and private provision, according to these three purposes.

DIAGRAM 2
A 'MAP' OF FINANCIAL PROVISION IN THE UK

PUBLIC	PRIVATE
REPLACEMENT OF EARNINGS eg Unemployment benefit Invalidity benefit Retirement pension	eg Occupational pension Employers' sick pay Mortgage protection policy
MEETING EXTRA NEEDS eg Child benefit Disability living allowance One parent benefit	eg House insurance Disability insurance
RELIEF OF POVERTY eg Income support Family credit Housing benefit	Charity

As we stressed earlier, every industrialised country operates a mix of different kinds of benefit. Diagram 3 provides a simplified comparison between benefits in the UK, Denmark, Germany and the USA. The models are not complete, nor completely accurate in their detail, but they provide a broad base for comparison. They do not permit any assessment of the size or weight of provision within each of the categories, but where provision is particularly significant it is presented in bold.

Diagram 3 begins to reveal the different balance of categorical, contributory and means-tested benefits in the different countries. In Germany, insurance benefits – where payment is conditional on contributions paid during employment – dominate provision. In Denmark, insurance and means-testing play a minor role, and most benefits are attached to particular conditions (eg unemployment, maternity) without any test of means or contributions. In the United States, means-tested benefits (known as 'welfare') play a major role in provision for poor families with children, but non means-tested, contributions-based pensions ('social security') are provided to retired people. Because the USA uses the same terms as the UK for entirely different systems, comparisons between the two countries are often misleading or simply wrong.

In practice, social security provision in most welfare capitalist countries is made up of a mixture of public and private provision, with the tax and benefits system including categorical, contributory and means-tested benefits. As in the UK, there is a fair amount of administrative and political complexity within the systems. The balance between different categories in different countries is the product of different policy priorities and different interpretations of the objectives of social security, as well as different political traditions and labour market conditions. Once we understand that every system is a mix of different kinds of benefit, it is easier to see that the mixture in the UK could be altered as part of a move towards modernising and reforming our welfare state.

DIAGRAM 3

Benefit Criteria	Britain	Denmark	Germany	United States
CONTINGENCY	Children Disability	Children Pension Sickness Maternity	Children	
CONTRIBUTION (insurance)	Pension Unemploymt Invalidity	Unemploymt	Unemploymt Pension Maternity	Old Age Sickness Disability Unemploymt
MEANS-TEST (assistance)	**Income support** Family Credit	Soc. Asst	Soc. Asst	**AFDC (children)** Supp. security
PRIVATE/ OCCUPATIONAL	**Pension** Sickness Maternity		Pension Sickness	**Pension** Sickness Maternity

Source: *Alcock,P (unpublished submission to the Commission on Social Justice)*

REFERENCES

Barr N (1988) *The Mirage of Private Unemployment Insurance* (London: LSE Welfare State Programme No.34).

Bennett F (1993) *Social Insurance: Reform or Abolition?* London, IPPR (Commission on Social Justice).

Falkingham J, Hills J, Lessof C (1993) *William Beveridge versus Robin Hood: Social Security and Redistribution over the Lifecycle* (London: LSE Welfare State Programme No.88).

Hills J (1993) *The Future of Welfare: a guide to the debate* (London: LSE/Joseph Rowntree Foundation).

THE COMMISSION ON SOCIAL JUSTICE
Terms of reference

The Commission on Social Justice was set up with the following terms of reference:

- To consider the principles of social justice and their application to the economic well-being of individuals and the community;

- To examine the relationship between social justice and other goals, including economic competitiveness and prosperity;

- To probe the changes in social and economic life over the last fifty years, and the failure of public policy to reflect them adequately; and to survey the changes that are likely in the foreseeable future, and the demands they will place on government;

- To analyse public policies, particularly in the fields of employment, taxation and social welfare, which could enable every individual to live free from want and to enjoy the fullest possible social and economic opportunities;

- And to examine the contribution which such policies could make to the creation of a fairer and more just society.

Membership

The 16 members of the Commission on Social Justice are:

Sir Gordon Borrie QC (Chair)	Former Director-General of Office of Fair Trading
Professor Tony Atkinson FBA	Professor of Political Economy, University of Cambridge
Anita Bhalla	Treasurer, Asian Resource Centre, Birmingham
Professor John Gennard	Professor of Industrial Relations, University of Strathclyde
Very Rev John Gladwin	Provost, Sheffield Cathedral
Christopher Haskins	Chief Executive, Northern Foods, PLC
Patricia Hewitt (Deputy Chair)	Deputy Director, IPPR
Dr Penelope Leach	President, Child Development Society
Professor Ruth Lister	Professor and Head of the Department of Applied Social Studies, University of Bradford
Emma MacLennan	Vice Chair, Low Pay Unit
Professor David Marquand	Professor of Politics, University of Sheffield
Bert Massie	Director, Royal Association for Disability and Rehabilitation
Dr Eithne McLaughlin	Lecturer in Social Policy, Queen's University, Belfast
Steven Webb	Economist, Institute for FiscalStudies
Margaret Wheeler	Director of Organisation Development, UNISON
Professor Bernard Williams	White's Professor of Moral Philosophy, University of Oxford

Evidence

The Commission has already received a large number of informal submissions from individuals and organisations about our remit, the problems we must confront, and the strategies we should adopt to solve them. We also know, however, that many organisations want to submit formal evidence to the Commission, covering their ideas for social reform, economic renewal and political change.

The Commission's first two discussion documents, The Justice Gap and Social Justice in a Changing World, set out some of the Commission's early thinking. The series of 'issue papers' (of which this publication is the second) are similarly intended to stimulate debate. Together the publications aim, at least in part, to help in the preparation of written evidence, which we welcome from any quarter. Evidence should, if possible, be sent to the Commission before the end of 1993. Oral hearings may be held, but none are yet planned.

Anyone wishing to contribute to the Commission's work can do so through its London or Glasgow offices. The addresses are:

Commission on Social Justice
Institute for Public Policy Research
30-32 Southampton Street
London
WC2E 7RA
Tel: 071 379 9400

Commission on Social Justice
c/c Centre for Housing Research
Glasgow University
25 Bute Gardens
Glasgow
G12 8RT
Tel: 041 339 8855 ext 4675